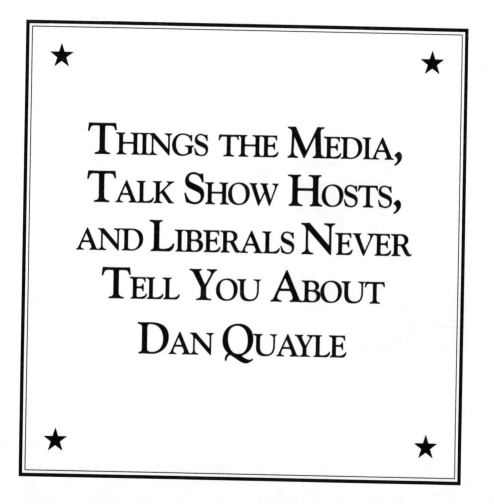

THINGS THE MEDIA, TALK SHOW HOSTS, AND LIBERALS NEVER TELL YOU ABOUT DAN QUAYLE

Star Song Publishing Group
  a division of Jubilee Communications, Inc.
P.O. Box 150009
Nashville, Tennessee 37215

ISBN 1-56233-040-3

Printed in the United States of America
First Printing, August 1992

1 2 3 4 5 6 7 8 9 9 97 96 95 94 93 92

TABLE OF CONTENTS

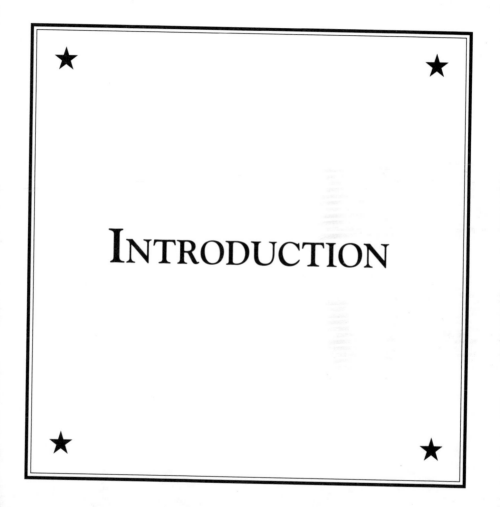

INTRODUCTION

I'm an average American. I'm a baby boomer who was born during the last days of the Eisenhower administration. I was raised in a loving family where positive values were instilled in my sister and me from an early age. I graduated from a small Midwestern college. I place my hand over my heart whenever I sing the National Anthem. I work hard Monday through Friday, putter around the house on Saturday, and go to church on Sunday. I've never been arrested for a crime. I don't cheat on my taxes. I send a donation to the local fire fighter's association each year. And, I live in a medium-sized city that is middle American both in terms of its geography and its attitudes.

I am unusual in one regard, however: My favorite course in college was Logic. As I began thinking about everything I had read and heard about Dan Quayle, it seemed very illogical that he could ascend to the second highest office in this country and possess the dubious qualities that his critics regularly allege. At the very least, I decided, he is a patient and forgiving man with a tremendous sense of humor — qualities that most Americans admire.

I thus embarked on a personal research project about the Vice President with the assistance of my mother, Wanda Mathews, a university librarian. What I discovered was a man of considerable depth, talent, foresight, and compassion. What I realized was that this is a Vice President who has performed his duties admirably under trying circumstances and with little fanfare. What I concluded was that Dan Quayle is an elected official who has served his country with distinction and integrity.

The purpose of this book is not to serve as an endorsement of one candidate or one party over another. Rather I hope it will simply help set the record straight about Vice President Quayle. By balancing the facts against satire and innuendo, voters will be able to make a more informed decision when they elect our country's leaders this fall. As an average American, I consider this right the greatest privilege in the world.

Jeanie Price
Nashville, Tennessee
1992

PROLOGUE

I was recently in Toledo, Ohio, and made what we call an impromptu visit to a Kroger's grocery store. While I was there I bought some of my favorite chocolate chip cookies. On the way out I offered a little girl one of the cookies. And you know what she said? She said, "My mommy told me not to take things from a stranger." And I said, "But I'm not a stranger. I'm the Vice President." And I can tell you this: for all the slings and arrows I've endured in the last four years, nothing has quite humbled me like that child's reply. "That's okay"—she told me, walking away—"I'm really not hungry anyway."

When you think about it, though, that little girl's suspicion of strangers tells us something sad about the world in which our children are growing up. Sure, mothers have always told their children to be wary of strangers. But you just have to pick up the newspaper on any given day to realize that in our world, that advice is a little more urgent.

In some ways we're a nation of strangers. And, as our society grows, maybe that's inevitable. We cannot—as the sophisticated folks are always reminding us—"turn back the clock" to the America of Norman Rockwell and the small-town values he celebrated. And yet those values are still there. They live in our communities, both large and small, where families get to know their neighbors, and where parents get to know their kids' teachers, the school bus driver, and the cop on the beat. They live in every home where parents patiently pass their experience and their values along to their children. These values live because they are invaluable. They stand as our essential guide to a good and honest life.

Now change is a permanent part of life. As Americans, we do not fear change—we're always confident we can shape our own future for the better—it's a matter of choice. But this means choosing wisely. It means realizing that some of the changes in our culture in recent decades have not been for the better. Some of these changes seem to have undermined the values we cherish.

In fact, these changes have created a cultural divide in our country. It is so great a divide that it sometimes seems we have two cultures—the cultural elite, and the rest of us. Most of us look at these social changes as we say, "Yes, change is inevitable, and much of it is good. But some of it is not. Let us preserve the good and reject the bad." And, my friends, most of us believe we should not be afraid to continue to talk about values—to try to judge what is right and what is wrong.

Yet, as I discovered recently, to appeal to our country's enduring, basic moral values is to invite the scorn and laughter of the elite culture. Talk about right and wrong, and they'll try to mock us in newsrooms, sitcom studios, and faculty lounges across America. But in the heart of America, in the homes and workplaces and churches, the message is heard. A sense of moral decency runs deep in American people. We know that the simple things, the simple gifts, and the simple truths that Americans have always sought to live by are more relevant than ever in our complex times. Among the sophisticates, to talk about simple moral principles is considered an embarrassng "gaffe." I guess that means they're embarrassed about the views of the average American—because moral values are what the American people care most about. And that's why I say this about the scorn of the media elite: "I wear their scorn as a badge of honor."

Vice President Dan Quayle
Excerpted from an address to the
Southern Baptists' Convention
June 9, 1992

ACCOMPLISHMENTS
OF DAN QUAYLE

★ ★

The "Quayle Amendment," passed in 1982, restored educational and other benefits to widows and children of service members killed in Vietnam.

★ ★

Although his congressional record was generally conservative, on matters of personal conviction he would occasionally cross ideological lines, voting to override President Reagan's veto of economic sanctions against South Africa, and he supported the creation of a national holiday honoring Martin Luther King, Jr.

Congress enacted legislation introduced by Quayle that deferred for 12 months student loan payments for pregnant women and recent mothers.

In 1976 he was asked by the Republican Party to enter what seemed to be a hopeless race in Indiana's fourth congressional district against an eight-term Democratic incumbent after the Republican candidate unexpectedly dropped out. Quayle won the election by capitalizing on his opponent's liberalism on social issues and his weakness on national defense.

_____

He was re-elected to Congress in 1978 by the largest margin ever in that district.

_____

During his four-year congressional tenure, he pushed through several amendments, including a prohibition on chemical and biological weapons testing near population centers, and a provision that the American hostages in Iran need not pay federal income tax during their captivity.

_____

In 1980, at the age of thirty-three, he became the youngest senator ever elected from the State of Indiana.

_____

He was the first Senator of his "class" elected in 1980 to have a bill enacted into law (an authorization for youth employment programs).

In 1982, he was the first member of the Senate to introduce a major tax-simplification bill. A similar bill was eventually enacted in 1986.

In 1982 he first introduced a proposal for a two-year federal budget cycle, designed to streamline the unwieldy congressional budget process.

A leader in student loan reform, Quayle introduced legislation to lower the default rate of student loans and to make a permanent provision of the tax law denying tax refunds to those who are in default on their student loans.

In 1984, Senator Quayle introduced a series of four measures on health care cost containment, resulting in the private sector Council on Health Care Technology, to assess the most beneficial and cost-effective use of medical technologies.

Senator Quayle authored legislation to provide more equitable treatment of rural hospitals in high-wage areas. This provision was signed into law with the Deficit Reduction Act of 1984.

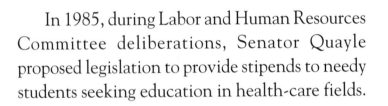

In 1985, during Labor and Human Resources Committee deliberations, Senator Quayle proposed legislation to provide stipends to needy students seeking education in health-care fields.

In 1985 and 1986, Senator Quayle introduced and won passage of legislation to promote arms cooperation with U.S. allies.

In 1986, he was re-elected to the Senate with 61% of the vote, the largest margin ever in Indiana.

Senator Quayle led the fight to redesign the budget process to make Congress more accountable for its actions and the President more able to fight pork barrel politics.

A leader on the issue of missile proliferation in the Third World, in 1986 Senator Quayle released the first of an annual series of Congressional Research Service reports on missile proliferation. These documents were the first comprehensive, unclassified reports of their kind.

———————————

While in the Senate, he was recognized as a capable and pragmatic politician, one who was willing to rise above partisan politics to achieve his legislative ends.

———————————

In pushing through the landmark Job Training and Partnership Act (JTPA) of 1982, he not only persuaded arch-rival Senator Edward Kennedy to cosponsor the bill, he also prevailed upon President Reagan to sign the bill into law.

By creating a program that responded to local job training needs, and most importantly emphasized the involvement of the private sector, the JTPA succeeded where Carter-era efforts had failed.

The JTPA sponsored by Quayle was so well conceived that 70% of its budget went directly to substantive job training, unlike the previous Comprehensive Employment and Training Act (CETA) which spent all but 11% of its budget on administrative and support costs.

The JTPA has placed over 3 million disadvantaged persons in private sector jobs. CETA, on the other hand, spent more than $52 million in nine years, but placed only 36% of its participants in permanent jobs, and only half of these were private sector jobs.

As a Senator, he served on the Budget Committee, the Armed Services Committee, and the Labor and Human Resources Committee.

★

As chairman of the Subcommittee on Defense Acquisition Policy he was the Senate leader in the drive to reform the Pentagon's purchasing practices, passing more than 60 amendments in this area.

★   ★

In his eight years in the Senate, he was considered by Democrats and Republicans to be a primary player in reforming the way the Department of Defense does business.

He guided into law initiatives to improve and extend federal programs to combat adult illiteracy.

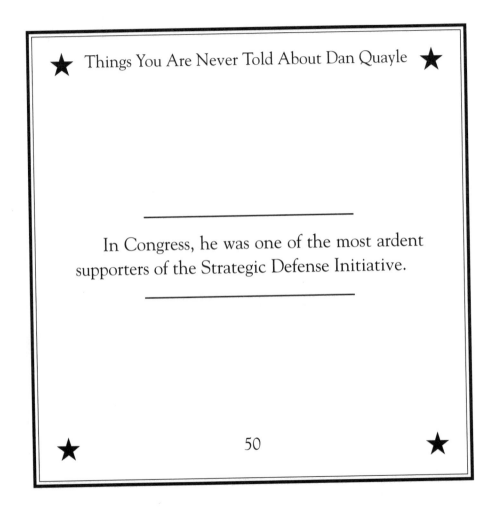

In Congress, he was one of the most ardent supporters of the Strategic Defense Initiative.

After pushing for clarification of certain points in the Intermediate-range Nuclear Forces Treaty (INF), he called for stricter verification procedures in future strategic arms treaties.

Senator Quayle persuaded the Department of Defense to adopt the crucial recommendations of his NATO Defense Initiative, which was designed to strengthen deterrence after the INF arms reductions took effect.

As Vice President, he has served as the chairman of the National Space Council and head of the President's Council on Economic Competitiveness.

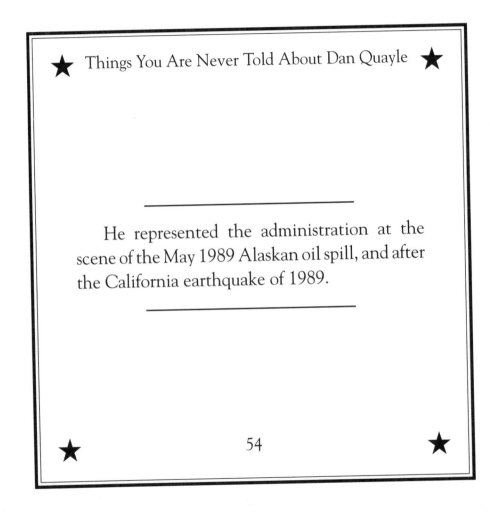

He represented the administration at the scene of the May 1989 Alaskan oil spill, and after the California earthquake of 1989.

He has surprised many members of the press because—unlike most politicians—he is able to discuss complex and technical information accurately without referring to notes or deferring to aides.

Although a member of the bar, he has sided with the American public in calling for legal reform, and an end to the "litigation-happy" civil justice system.

★ ★

_____

Shortly after Iraq invaded Kuwait, the White House sent him to South America to push for increased oil production, and to halt the transfer of ballistic missile technology to Iraq. He successfully achieved both of these difficult yet secret missions.

_____

He is known around the White House as being quick, well-read, and hardworking.

He has been given at least as much responsibility and access to White House decision making as his two predecessors, George Bush and Walter Mondale—the two most powerful vice presidents in history.

_____

He is one of President Bush's key strategists on both long- and short-term legislative priorities for the Administration.

_____

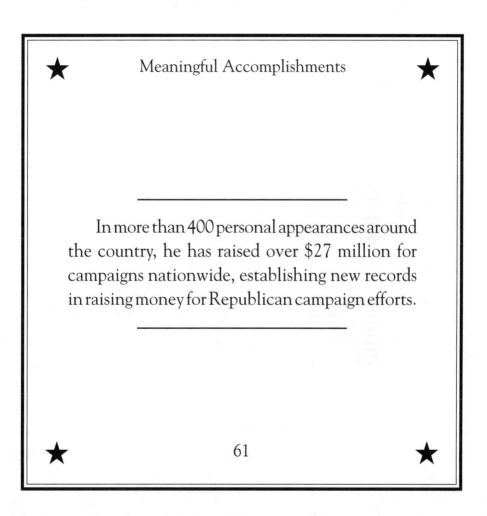

In more than 400 personal appearances around the country, he has raised over $27 million for campaigns nationwide, establishing new records in raising money for Republican campaign efforts.

He is the first vice president to deploy resources on behalf of GOP state legislative candidates, in anticipation of the post-1990 redistricting.

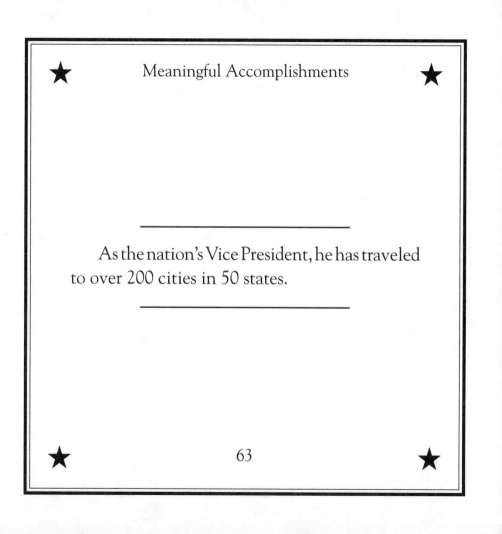

Meaningful Accomplishments

As the nation's Vice President, he has traveled to over 200 cities in 50 states.

He has conducted more than 600 interviews and press conferences and 32 editorial board meetings to discuss Administration policy.

★

He has become one of the strongest voices on behalf of school choice, meeting with parents, teachers, and education reform activists across the country.

───────────────

He has visited 47 countries to promote U.S. interests.

───────────────

★ ★

★ ★

By holding more than 300 meetings with
visiting foreign leaders in his Washington office
and joining President Bush in numerous Oval
Office diplomatic sessions, he has handled more
than his share of foreign policy development.

★ ★

While in El Salvador, February 1989, he urged Salvadoran leaders to participate in free and fair elections. He also warned the Salvadoran military about human rights violations.

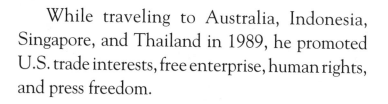

While traveling to Australia, Indonesia, Singapore, and Thailand in 1989, he promoted U.S. trade interests, free enterprise, human rights, and press freedom.

In June of 1989 he successfully urged Central American leaders to push for fair elections in Nicaragua.

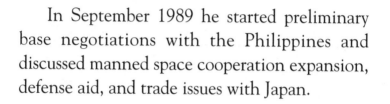

In September 1989 he started preliminary base negotiations with the Philippines and discussed manned space cooperation expansion, defense aid, and trade issues with Japan.

In March 1990 he assisted in starting the demilitarization/demobilization process for Nicaragua through talks with Latin American leaders.

In April 1990 he traveled to Nicaragua and Mexico. There he discussed economic development and U.S. economic relief assistance. He consulted with Mexican President Salinas on the drug war and obstacles to peace in Central America. He also consulted with Latin American leaders regarding events in Panama.

In May 1990 he traveled to Italy, Great Britain, and France. While there he consulted with European leaders on the future of NATO and economic cooperation; he also discussed commercialization and exploration of space with the European Space Agency.

In December 1990 and January 1991 he met with troops deployed to Saudi Arabia as part of Operation Desert Shield and discussed options and financial arrangements for funding U.S. participation in the Gulf crisis with Kuwaiti and Saudi leaders.

As the highest ranking American ever to visit the three newly independent Baltic states (Estonia, Latvia, and Lithuania), he focused on European security, economic relations, and the importance of human rights.

As Chairman of the President's Council on Competitiveness, he announced the Administration's Agenda for Civil Justice Reform at the American Bar Association's 1991 Convention, and proposed 50 far-reaching reforms of America's judicial system that will reduce excessive litigation. Also under his direction, the Council formed the Administration's consensus position in favor of product liability reform legislation, which is now pending before Congress.

Under his direction the Competitiveness Council published a report on biotechnology that outlines—for the first time—Administration policy to support free market development of the fledgling biotechnology industry.

He spearheaded the Administration's efforts to protect property rights from encroachment by excessive regulations. In addition, the Vice President has strongly supported legislation (S.50) that would give landowners a right to sue when agencies fail to protect private property rights in their procedures.

He announced the Competitiveness Council's package of far-reaching reforms of the Food and Drug Administration's drug approval process. These reforms will ensure that patients who suffer from serious and life threatening diseases, such as AIDS, cancer, and Alzheimer's disease, have access to promising new drugs as soon as possible. The initiative ensures that the government review process does not delay the availability of safe and effective drugs for all Americans.

★　　　　　　　　　　　　　　　　　　★

He chaired the Competitiveness Council's deliberation on the Wetlands Delineation Manual that restored a proper balance to the wetlands land-use regulations.

He has announced that the Competitiveness Council will outline a comprehensive, future-oriented approach for government telecommunications policy into the 21st century and completed a thorough study of the economic benefits to American consumers of deregulation in the 1980s.

    As chairman of the National Space Council, he has personally and directly reinvigorated and restructured the nation's space program.

He has pushed for changes and established long-term civil space goals built around two initiatives: Mission to Planet Earth and Mission from Plant Earth.

The space council is now managing the space program as a national effort, taking advantage of competition and collaboration. He has successfully prodded federal agencies to find faster, cheaper, and better ways of doing things in space by applying the cutting edge ideas of one agency to another. One important result was the Council's restructuring of NASA's Earth Observing System (EOS)—a program to measure global climate change—borrowing on technical ideas from the Energy and Defense Departments.

He restructured the EOS program, breaking its large, expensive satellites into smaller units to get results on global warming faster and with less risk.

He developed a national launch system to provide low-cost reliable access to space.

He decided against building additional space shuttle orbiters and he restructured the Space Station program to reduce cost and risk.

In restructuring the EOS program he also developed a comprehensive new commercial space policy to ensure a competitive and healthy U.S. commercial space industry.

He brought the Departments of Defense and Energy, along with NASA, into President Bush's Space Exploration Initiative.

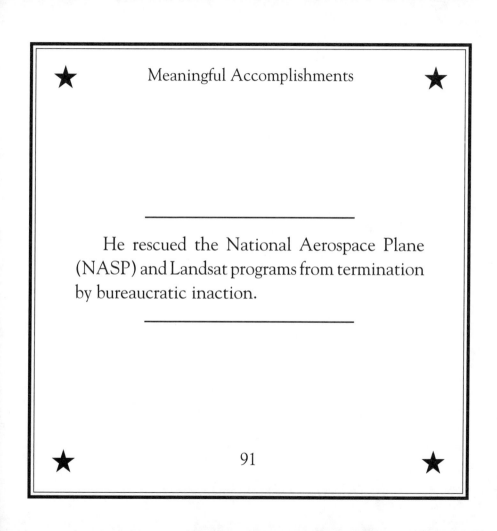

Meaningful Accomplishments

He rescued the National Aerospace Plane (NASP) and Landsat programs from termination by bureaucratic inaction.

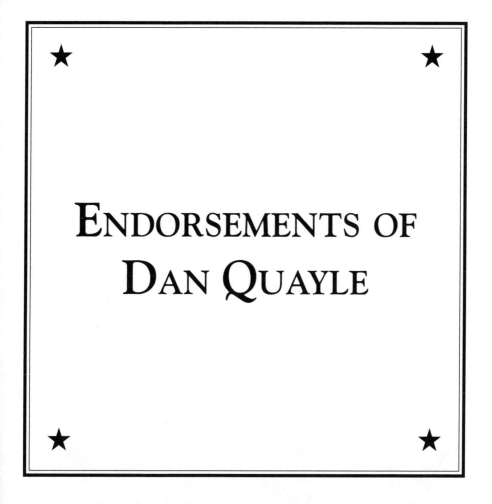

ENDORSEMENTS OF
DAN QUAYLE

———————————

Despite attacks from the press and political opponents, Dan Quayle still has the full support of George Bush who has said, "I see him in action, I know what he's doing. He has been extraordinarily helpful, and I can't ask any more of him."

———————————

Before his resignation, former White House Chief of Staff John Sununu said, "When we lay out a legislative strategy, almost automatically [Dan Quayle's] a key part of the discussions."

★ ★

Former White House Chief of Staff Samuel Skinner said, "Number one, his basic values are right. Number two, his political judgement is solid. Number three, he is not wrapped up in the trappings of the office . . . . And number four, while he's young . . . he has had an experience that is very significant.

Abe Rosenthal, former editor of the *New York Times*, stated, "I think Mr. Quayle is far more able and sophisticated than he is drawn in the press and on TV. So do politicians and legislators I respect of both parties."

Dennis DeConcini, senior Democrat senator from Arizona, said, "Whatever one thinks of Dan Quayle's politics, the argument that he is unqualified to be President is ridiculous and the press knows it . . . . It's time that we give Vice President Quayle the respect he is entitled to, not just because of the office, but because of the individual that he is."

According to Thomas DiBacco, a historian at American University, the vice president compares very favorably to most of his predecessors. "Quayle is probably better prepared for assuming responsibilities under the 25th Amendment than most No. 2 men in history. President Bush has kept him involved and briefed and their relationship appears not only cordial but a model of professionalism between high-level executives."

In January of 1991, the Gannett News Service reported that "One former U.S. Senator who deserves a lot of credit for the improved version of the Patriot missile is Vice President Quayle. . . . It was Quayle who fought to make sure the Pentagon followed through."

Sara Fritz, staff writer for *The Los Angeles Times*, observed in a May 1991 article: "By all accounts, Quayle has acquitted himself admirably as Vice President. He has been a loyal advisor at the White House, and effective partisan on the stump, a competent diplomat on foreign assignments, and a persuasive advocate on Capitol Hill. The trouble is, few people have been paying much attention."

According to *Time*, "He does not sit quietly at Cabinet meetings . . . . Instead he injects his opinion frequently, often disagreeing with Administration heavyweights."

In a *Newsday* article Richard Viguerie wrote "For 33 months [Quayle] has maintained his composure in the face of ridicule that would have broken the heart of a lesser man. . . . He has rarely had an unkind word to say about anybody."

★ ★

Charles Krauthammer wrote in *The Washington Post* "I don't know one who could have matched for depth and dexterity the two-hour analysis of the Intermediate Nuclear Force Treaty that Quayle offered when I first encountered him in April 1988."

★ ★

_____

In a 1991 column, Paul Harvey points out that Dan Quayle "has never been one of the good ol' boys socially, preferring to excuse himself from most D.C. party-hopping in favor of spending time with his wife and their three teen-age children."

_____

———————————

Former White House Chief of Staff Samuel Skinner said, "George Bush does not like to have people on his team who are petty, who are cheap-shot artists. He wants . . . people who think of others. And Dan Quayle fits that category."

———————————

David Rockefeller on Dan Quayle in Latin America: "I don't think the U.S. could have been better represented than by the Vice President."

★ ★

After a visit from Quayle in June 1991, German Chancellor Helmut Kohl told aides he thought Quayle had an impressive grasp of global issues, and that he wondered why Quayle received such negative press in the U.S.

According to Forbes magazine, "Dan Quayle is not the Dan Quayle portrayed by political commentators and TV comedians. And never has been."

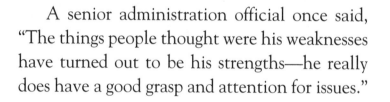

A senior administration official once said, "The things people thought were his weaknesses have turned out to be his strengths—he really does have a good grasp and attention for issues."

The *Almanac of American Politicians* wrote: "In the Senate, Quayle has been one of the most successful members of the Republican class of 1980."

★ ★

★ ★

According to Texas Senator John Tower, Quayle's performance during the Intermediate-range Nuclear Forces (INF) Treaty was the "clearest indication" that he is a man willing "to put principle before political expediency."

During the INF debate Senator John McCain stated, "Senator Quayle . . . has done such enormous and painstaking work, becoming one of the leaders in this body, and indeed the nation, on defense issues and our strategic challenges."

During his tenure in the Senate, a writer for the *Wall Street Journal* stated, "One of the better ideas we've seen so far is the NATO Defense Initiative being promoted around Washington by Senator Dan Quayle. . . . That strategy calls for a flexible, mobile force that doesn't have to 'go nuclear' as soon as the East's forces 'go nuclear.' The fact that serious people are considering such things is encouraging news for NATO."

Kenneth Adelman (former Director of the U.S. Arms Control and Disarmament Agency) stated, "The Job Training Partnership Act [developed by Dan Quayle] turned around the federal government's 8 billion yearly program of make-work, public sector jobs. Displaced workers were placed in tax-paying, rather than tax-eating positions."

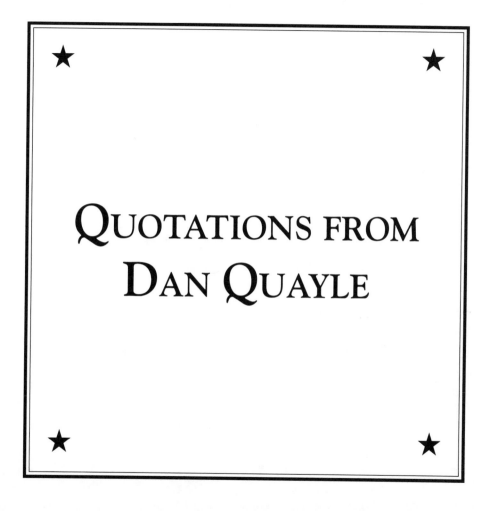

QUOTATIONS FROM
DAN QUAYLE

Like so many Americans, for me, family comes first. When family values are undermined, our country suffers. All too often, parents struggle to instill character in their sons and daughters, only to see their values belittled and their beliefs mocked by those who look down on America. Americans try to raise their children to understand right and wrong, only to be told that every so-called "life-style alternative" is morally equivalent. That is wrong.

A lot of politics is timing. Timing and opportunity. And the two are critical to success, but you can't necessarily determine either one of them.

We should not be afraid to continue to talk about values—to try to judge what is right and what is wrong.

The cultural elite in Hollywood and elsewhere may have a lot of money; they may have a lot of influence. But we have the power of ideas, the power of our convictions, and the power of our beliefs.

If America ever lost its moral vision, it would cease to be America. To paraphrase my grandfather, I would say that America is good because America is free. But he understood that it works the other way around, too: that if America ceased to be good, it would cease to be free. We would become a soulless and divided nation, a nation under siege instead of a nation under God. Our common vision of the good and just life is what keeps the "united" in "United States."

Confronted with life's great moral issues, a sneer is not an answer.

Those who turn away from moral truths restrict themselves. I know it is politically correct to be dismissive of those who speak of moral values. But political correctness is a form of intolerance.

Renewal, ultimately, is not primarily the work of government. It's our work, the work of our churches, the work of each person, responding each day to the hard questions of life and faith. It's the work of choosing wisely. Choosing to live in falsehood or in fidelity. Choosing to follow man in his foolish ways or the Son of Man who walked the way of love and mercy, full of grace and truth.

Our diversity is our strength.

There is no question that this country has had a terrible problem with race and racism. The evil of slavery has left a long legacy. But we have faced racism squarely, and we have made progress in the past quarter century .... There is more to be done. But I think that all of us can be proud of our progress.

_____

If we as a society don't condemn what is wrong, how can we teach our children what is right?

_____

I believe the lawless social anarchy which we saw [during the L. A. riots] is directly related to the breakdown of family structure, personal responsibility, and social order in too many areas of society.

For the government, transforming underclass culture means that our policies and programs must create a different incentive system. Our policies must be premised on, and must reinforce, values such as family, hard work, integrity, and personal responsibility.

We are for law and order. If a single mother raising her children in the ghetto has to worry about drive-by shootings, drug deals, or whether her children will join gangs and die violently, her difficult task becomes impossible. We are for law and order because we can't expect children to learn in dangerous schools. We are for law and order because if property isn't protected, who will build businesses?

Our urban agenda includes fully funding the Home-ownership Opportunity for People Everywhere program. HOPE—as we call it—will help public housing residents become home owners. Subsidized housing all too often merely made rich investors richer. Home ownership will give the poor a stake in their neighborhoods, and a chance to build equity.

Our urban agenda includes creating enterprise zones by slashing taxes in targeted areas, including a zero capital gains tax, to spur entrepreneurship, economic development, and job creation in the inner cities.

Our urban agenda includes instituting our education strategy, America 2000, to raise academic standards and to give the poor the same choices about how and where to educate their children that rich people have.

Our urban agenda includes welfare reform to remove the penalties for marriage, create incentives for saving, and give communities greater control over how the programs are administered.

Empowering the poor will strengthen families. And right now, the failure of our families is hurting America deeply.

When families fail, society fails.

The anarchy and lack of structure in our inner cities are testament to how quickly civilization falls apart when the family foundation cracks.

Children need love and discipline. They need mothers and fathers.

A welfare check is not a husband. The state is not a father.

It is from parents that children learn how to behave in society; it is from parents above all that children come to understand values and themselves as men and women, mothers and fathers.

It's time to talk again about family, hard work, integrity, and personal responsibility. We cannot be embarrassed out of belief that two parents, married to each other, are better in most cases for children than one. That honest work is better than handouts or crime. That we are our brothers' keepers. That it's worth making an effort, even when the rewards aren't immediate.

———————————————

We are, as our children recite each morning, "one nation under God." That's a useful framework for acknowledging a duty and an authority higher than our own pleasures and personal ambitions.

———————————————

Unless we change the basic rules of society— in our inner cities and, for that matter, among many more fortunate Americans—we cannot expect anything else to change for the better. This requires the hardest kind of change: not just economic, not just political, but cultural change. A change of values—and thereby, a change in individual behavior.

Renewing our commitment to Judeo-Christian values has to come in our churches and synagogues, our civic organizations, and our schools. Most of all, it has to come in our homes. For if values are not firmly grounded there, they will never take root elsewhere. But, on the other hand, if we revive in our families, the lights of conscience, commitment, and compassion, then our homes will be beacons in stormy times, showing a brighter and safer way, especially for young people, into the future.

For two decades now, the overwhelming emphasis of the national media has been in favor of abortion. That is why, 19 years after *Roe* v. *Wade* was decided, the American people are still being told that it just "legalized abortion in the first trimester," when, in fact, *Roe* had the effect of permitting unrestricted abortion through all nine months of pregnancy. That struck at the fundamental value of all American society: the value of human life.

When the full implications of *Roe* are explained to the American people, they reject that decision. In poll after poll, the majority of Americans support limitations on abortion. Let's look at the Pennsylvania statute . . . . That law provides time for reflection before an irrevocable decision. It calls for a 24-hour waiting period, spousal notification, and parental consent for minor children. That law was passed with bipartisan support and signed by a Democratic governor.

The pro-life movement—uniting Americans of all races and faiths—is committed to tolerance. The pro-life movement—defending the unborn, the handicapped, the terminally ill—is committed to compassion. But compassion does not mean moral neutrality. Tolerance does not mean abandoning our most cherished convictions. And it surely does not mean remaining silent and passive in the face of cruelty and injustice.

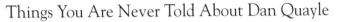

Our solution, for those mothers who feel they cannot raise the child, is adoption. Our opponents treat God's greatest gift—new life—as an inconvenience to be discarded. But we believe life is a beautiful gift to be cherished and cared for—however "inconvenient" its beginning may be.

Whatever the disagreements in American society today, whatever our divisions, whatever our anger or disappointment with one another, we don't take it out on the kids.

One reason our schools are in a crisis is because they have, in many ways, lost their moral bearings. When eighth graders are squandering the gift of youthful innocence in premarital sex—the solution is not to give them a condom. The solution is to give them value-based education. To teach them what is right and wrong. To teach them that they and they alone are responsible for their actions.

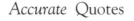

Public school educators should be less concerned with promoting "life-styles" curricula, and more concerned with teaching basic values—personal integrity, responsibility, hard work, and morality—to their students.

When children are more likely to encounter a drug pusher in the school hallway than a wise teacher it's not enough to post "Drug Free" signs on the building and warn them of the dangers they risk. Those are helpful, but not enough. The only true solution is to instill in our children a sense of *their own* value. And no anti-drug law or abortion counsellor or sex-education manual can teach a child to value himself or herself.

There is only one school of life's true values, and that is the family—especially the *traditional family*. If our country and its cities remain strong, it will be because our families and their values will remain strong.

I am not saying everyone should make the same choices I have. But whatever we decide in life—whether it's staying single, getting married, deciding to have children, and then choosing how much we'll be involved in what they do—whatever we decide, we then have responsibilities. If a young girl becomes pregnant, she has made a choice and now has a responsibility; the same is true for the boy. No person can ever say the consequences of his or her actions are someone else's responsibility.

When we talk about basic values, we're talking about faith. Hard work. Personal responsibility. Integrity. Knowing right from wrong. A child raised according to those values by a strong parent or parents will have a better chance of making it than one who doesn't have those advantages.

A child who receives a value-based education will be better prepared for the demands and the trials of life. That will be even more true where the parents are involved with what goes on in the school. Where our kids are concerned, we do not have one minute to waste—and that is why we support reforms that will give the parents the right to choose where their children go to school.

Character is always an issue when we decide who will hold the highest office in our land. Character is leadership: what you will do under fire; how you will handle tough decisions.

We need jobs, not make-work, pork barrel. Only the private sector can create real jobs that employ people to make real products and real services that people need and can be proud of.

I beleve that the Bush Administration's empowerment agenda will help the poor gain power, by creating opportunity, and letting people make the choices that free citizens must make.

The ideals of the republic remain unchanged: the rights of the individual are fundamental in America. We take rights seriously.

We believe economic growth is achieved through the basic principles of opportunity, entrepreneurship, and the free market. Economic growth comes from our people, and not from government.

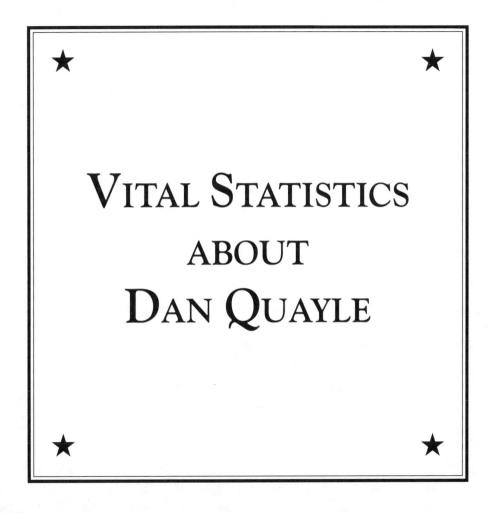

VITAL STATISTICS
ABOUT
DAN QUAYLE

James Danforth Quayle was born on February 4, 1947 in Indianapolis, Indiana.

★ ★ ★

He married Marilyn Tucker, a fellow law student whose accumulation of Girl Scout Honor badges had earned her the nickname "Merit."

★ ★ ★

The Quayles have three children—Tucker Danforth, Benjamin Eugene, and Mary Corrine.

★ ★ ★

His maternal grandfather owned five newspapers in Indiana and two in Arizona, where he was a frequent champion of conservative causes and known as "the founding father of the Republican party in Arizona."

★ ★ ★

During high school, he often attended rallies for local Republican candidates and stood on street corners distributing campaign literature.

★ ★ ★

While in school, he was popular among his peers, with whom he played golf and basketball, and cruised in his car with vanity plates reading AuH2O (the chemical symbol for Barry Goldwater's surname).

★ ★ ★

While a student at DePauw college in Greencastle, Indiana, he majored in political science, captained the golf team, and was the president of Delta Kappa Epsilon (the same fraternity as his father, grandfather, and George Bush).

★ ★ ★

169

As a student he earned spending money by waiting tables and working at his father's newspaper as a pressman and court reporter during summer vacations.

★ ★ ★

During the 1968 Republican Convention in Miami Beach, Florida, he was a driver for the Nixon entourage.

★ ★ ★

In 1971 he was an investigator with the Consumer Protection Division of the attorney general's office.

★ ★ ★

He served as an administrative assistant to Indiana Governor Edgar Whitcomb.

★ ★ ★

From 1973 to 1974 he served as the director of the Inheritance Tax Division of the Indiana Department of Revenue.

★ ★ ★

He managed a family-owned newspaper while sharing a law practice with his wife before his election to the House of Representatives in 1976.

His first political involvement was at the Arizona state fair where he handed out leaflets for his grandfather's good friend, Barry Goldwater.

★ ★ ★

As the wife of the Vice President, Marilyn Quayle has been an active volunteer for disaster-relief efforts.

★ ★ ★

In the July/August 1992 issue of *Today's Christian Woman*, Marilyn Quayle is quoted as saying, "I always try to look at the decisions I make and ask myself, 'Is this what Christ would have done?' Sometimes the answer is no, and I'm mad at myself. Walking with Christ is just that—a walk. I know I'm not perfect, and I try not to be disappointed in myself. I also believe joy is the greatest living testimony for a Christian. How can you be a testimony if your life is without joy?"

★ ★ ★

According to Quayle getting married made him very serious about life, and gave him a stronger sense of where he wanted to go and what he wanted to do.

★ ★ ★

Dan Quayle is the 44th Vice President of the United States.

★ ★ ★